FIRST 15 LESSONS
MANDOLIN

by Fred Sokolow

Includes Audio & Video Access

2 LESSON 1
Parts of the Mandolin
Tuning the Mandolin
Holding the Mandolin and Pick
Mandolin Tab and Chord Grids

4 LESSON 2
Easy Chords, Key of G
A Shuffle Beat Strum
G Major Scale
Playing a Melody

6 LESSON 3
Chords for the Key of D
A Rock (Straight-Eighths) Strum
D Major Scale
Playing a Melody

8 LESSON 4
Key of A Chords
A Rock Ballad Strum
A Major Scale
Playing a Melody
"Sawing" (Filling out a Melody)

10 LESSON 5
Key of C Chords
A 6/8 Strum
Arpeggios
C Major Scale
Playing a Melody

12 LESSON 6
Key of E Chords
A Waltz Strum
E Major Scale
Playing a Melody

14 LESSON 7
Key of F Chords
A Latin/R&B Strum
F Major Scale
Playing a Melody

16 LESSON 8
Tremolo
Double Stops in Several Keys
Tremolo with Double Stops
"Will the Circle Be Unbroken"

18 LESSON 9
Chop Chords
Moveable Chop Chord Families
Chop Chord Major Scales

20 LESSON 10
Seventh Chords
The 12-Bar Blues
Blues Soloing

22 LESSON 11
Fancier Chords (First Position)
Major 7ths
Diminished Chords
Augmented Chords
Minor 6ths
Suspended Chords

24 LESSON 12
Moveable Chords
Moveable Chord Families

26 LESSON 13
Blues Chords: Moveable 9ths and 7ths
Moveable Blues Chord Families
Moveable Minor Pentatonic Scales

28 LESSON 14
Navigating the Circle-of-Fifths
The Rhythm Changes

30 LESSON 15
Chord/Melody Playing
"The Godfather (Love Theme)"

32 ABOUT THE AUTHOR

PLAYBACK+
Speed Pitch Balance Loop

To access audio, video, and extra content visit:
www.halleonard.com/mylibrary

Enter Code
6777-6722-1948-3717

ISBN 978-1-5400-4602-4

HAL•LEONARD®

Visit Hal Leonard Online at
www.halleonard.com

Contact Us:
Hal Leonard
7777 West Bluemound Road
Milwaukee, WI 53213
Email: info@halleonard.com

In Europe contact:
Hal Leonard Europe Limited
42 Wigmore Street
Marylebone, London, W1U 2RN
Email: info@halleonardeurope.com

In Australia contact:
Hal Leonard Australia Pty. Ltd.
4 Lentara Court
Cheltenham, Victoria, 3192 Australia
Email: info@halleonard.com.au

Before you start playing, here are some basic facts you need to know:

PARTS OF THE MANDOLIN

 Mandolins come in three different shapes: The F model (preferred by bluegrass players); the A model; and the roundback, or Neapolitan style, also called the "tater bug." Except for the F model's "scroll" and "points," all three styles have similar parts.

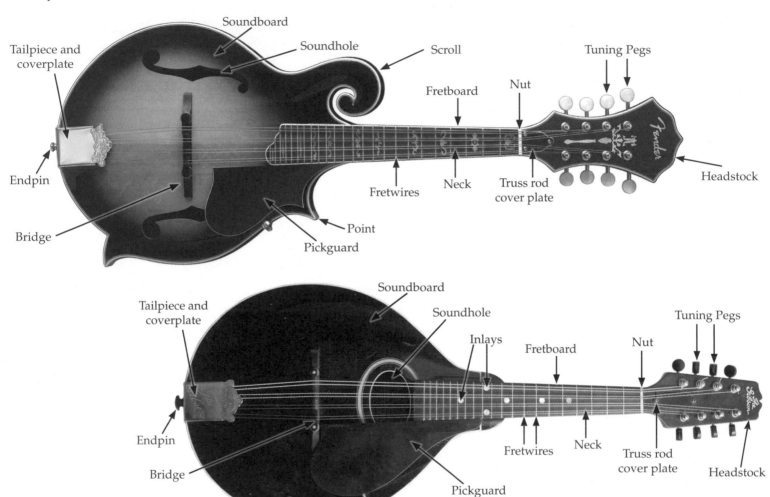

TUNING THE MANDOLIN

 A free online tuner comes with this book! Visit www.halleonard.com/mylibrary and enter the code found on page 1 to access it.

Electronic tuners are helpful. The most convenient tuners clip on the mandolin's headstock and read the strings' vibrations.

The mandolin has four pairs (or courses) of strings: Each pair is tuned in unison and is referred to as if it were a single string. For example, the two lightest strings are both tuned to a high E and are called "the first string." Both strings of each course are played simultaneously. The mandolin is tuned in fifths, like a violin. From lowest (thickest) to highest (thinnest) strings, the tuning is:

G-D-A-E

Pluck a string and twist its tuning peg to match the desired pitch. For the fourth and third pairs, turn the tuning peg clockwise to lower the string's pitch and counterclockwise to raise it; for the second and first pairs, turn the tuning pegs in the opposite directions.

HOLDING THE MANDOLIN AND PICK

The illustrations show comfortable positions for sitting or standing with the mandolin. Notice the position of the strap, which makes standing with the instrument easier.

Most mandolin players use a thick, heavy pick. There are three preferred shapes:

MANDOLIN TAB AND CHORD GRIDS

In tablature ("tab" for short), the lines represent strings and the numbers are frets. Here's a sample:

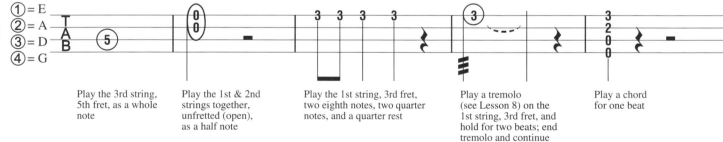

Play the 3rd string, 5th fret, as a whole note

Play the 1st & 2nd strings together, unfretted (open), as a half note

Play the 1st string, 3rd fret, two eighth notes, two quarter notes, and a quarter rest

Play a tremolo (see Lesson 8) on the 1st string, 3rd fret, and hold for two beats; end tremolo and continue to hold for one quarter note

Play a chord for one beat

Chord grids are pictures of the fretboard. Compare the grid to the photo of a chord.

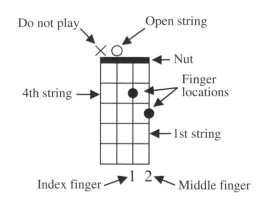

3

EASY CHORDS, KEY OF G

The language of music is often expressed with numbers rather than letters. Musicians say, "Go to the 4 chord," or "Go to the 2 minor." The numbers refer to steps of the major scale. Since C is the first note in the C major scale, a C chord is the 1 chord in the key of C. The 2 chord is D (or Dm or D7), and so on.

Regardless of a song's key, the 1, 4, and 5 chords are the chords that are most likely to occur. Millions of folk, country, blues, bluegrass, and classic rock songs consist of just those three chords. In the key of G, G is 1, C is 4, and D is 5.

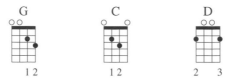

Practice playing each chord, then practice switching from one chord to another. Notice that it's easy to go from G to C or vice-versa: you hold the two-finger position and simply move it up or down a string. So, to go from G to C, move your index and middle fingers "over" from the first and second strings to the second and third strings.

A SHUFFLE BEAT STRUM

This strum will serve you well in many musical genres. The diagram below shows how to play a single bar (four beats) of shuffle beat. ⊓ represents a downstroke, and ⋁ is an upstroke.

Strum a G chord:

⊓	—	⊓	⋁	⊓	—	⊓	⋁
1	and	2	and	3	and	4	and

Notice that you don't hit the strings on the "and" of 1 or the "and" of 3. However, your hand still moves in an up-stroke motion in order to keep a constant "down-up-down-up" motion going. This is known as a "ghost" stroke.

Play the following snippet of "I Am a Man of Constant Sorrow" to practice strumming the shuffle beat and changing chords.

"I Am a Man of Constant Sorrow"

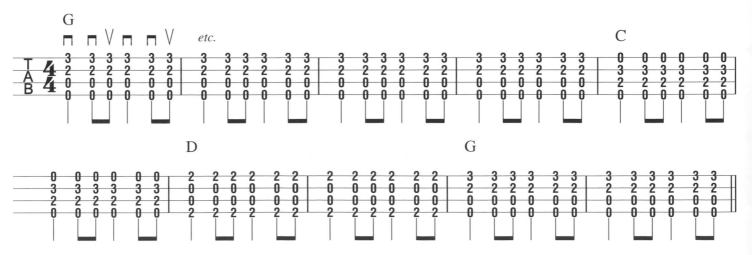

If a song includes more chords than the 1-4-5 chord family, the most likely chords are the relative minors of 1, 4, or 5. Every major chord has a *relative minor* (a closely related chord that is a sixth higher). In the key of G, the relative minors are: Em (relative minor of G), Am (relative minor of C) and Bm (relative minor of D).

In the following diagrams, the arc connecting two dots indicates a *barre*—play both strings with your index finger.

Practice playing the three minor chords, then play this exercise that makes use of them:

Play the following fragment of the bluegrass/country hit "Rocky Top" to practice a fast shuffle beat and make use of one of the relative minor chords in the key of G (Em).

"Rocky Top"

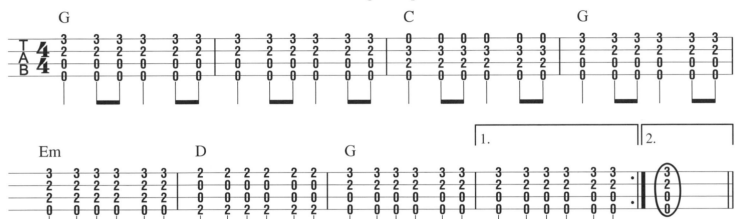

G MAJOR SCALE

The more familiar you are with major scales, the easier it will be to pick out melodies. Play the G major scale up and down in a loop, as it's written below, using the fingering indicated on the fretboard chart. Start on a downstroke, and alternate downstrokes and upstrokes:

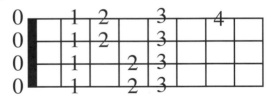

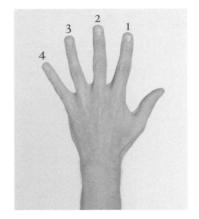

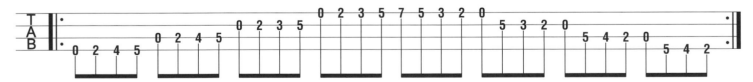

PLAYING A MELODY

Practice the G major scale, then try playing simple melodies like "Twinkle, Twinkle, Little Star," "This Land is Your Land," or "Take Me Out to the Ball Game."

"Take Me Out to the Ball Game"

etc.

CHORDS FOR THE KEY OF D

The D chord family consists of D (1), G (4), A (5), and their relative minors: Bm, Em, and F#m. Most of these chords were in Lesson 2. Here are the new chords and an exercise to help you practice them:

A ROCK (STRAIGHT-EIGHTHS) STRUM

A staple in rock music, the *straight-eighths* rhythm, has eight beats to a bar; and unlike in a shuffle beat, all the beats are more equal in emphasis. On the mandolin, this rhythm can be played with downstrokes, or with upstrokes and downstrokes for a more relaxed strum. Play a D chord and practice both strums:

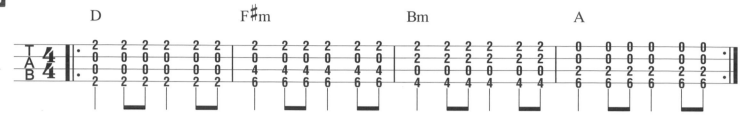

Use both versions of the straight-eighths strum to play the following exercise. It'll help you practice the new chord family.

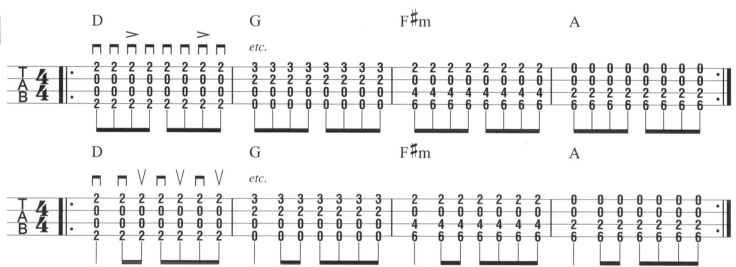

The Byrds' version of the iconic Bob Dylan song "Mr. Tambourine Man" features a straight-eighths beat. Play this portion of the tune using the more relaxed strum:

"Mr. Tambourine Man"

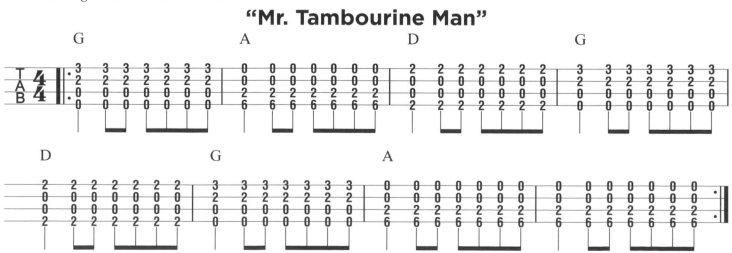

The following eight bars of Rod Stewart's "Maggie May" have a straight-eighths feel and make use of the extended D chord family: 1, 4, and 5, plus a few of the relative minors.

"Maggie May"

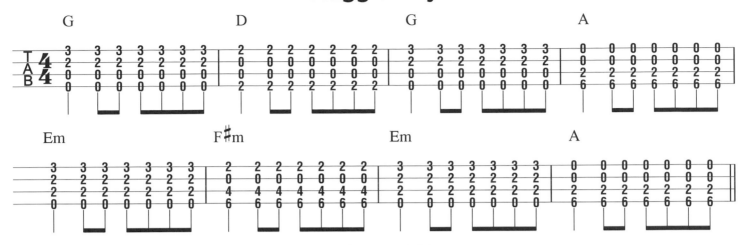

D MAJOR SCALE

Practice the D major scale by playing it in a loop, as written below.

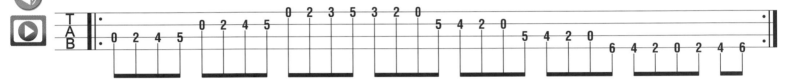

PLAYING A MELODY

Fiddle tunes are a mainstay of bluegrass and old-time music; and most of them are based on the major scale so they make good exercises for learning the scales. "Arkansas Traveler" is one of the world's most popular fiddle tunes. When you play it, pick down on the downbeats and up on the upbeats:

"Arkansas Traveler"

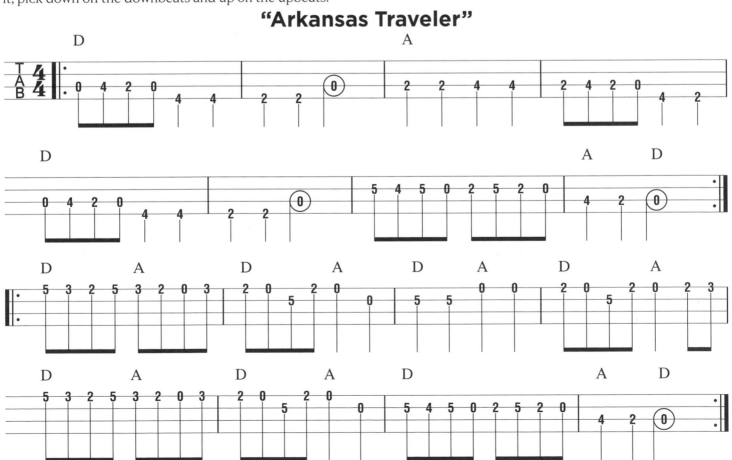

KEY OF A CHORDS

The A chord family is A (1), D (4), and E (5). The relative minors are F#m, Bm, and C#m. E7 is an easier chord than E, so we'll go with that for now. (The 5 chord can almost always be a seventh chord as well as a major chord.) Here are the new chord shapes and an exercise to help you practice them:

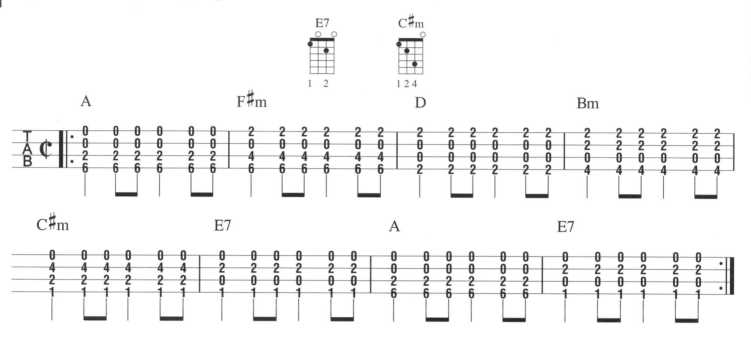

A ROCK BALLAD STRUM

Here's yet another rhythmic feel, one you need to play classic rock tunes like "Hey Jude," "Free Bird," or Neil Young's "Helpless." The beats are divided into sixteenth notes instead of eighth notes:

Strum an A chord:

⊓	—	⊓	V	⊓	—	⊓	V	⊓	—	⊓	V	⊓	V	⊓	V
1	a	and	a	2	a	and	a	3	a	and	a	4	a	and	a

Let's put that to use and play a bit of Bob Dylan's "Knockin' on Heaven's Door."

"Knockin' on Heaven's Door"

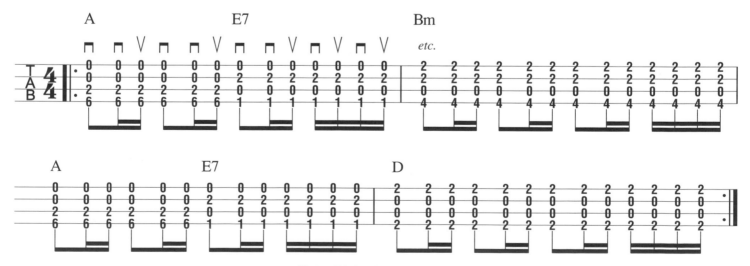

A MAJOR SCALE

Practice the A major scale as written, and don't forget to start with a downstroke and continue with alternating downstrokes and upstrokes:

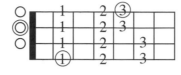

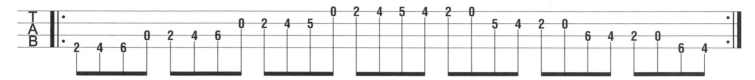

PLAYING A MELODY

"Sailors Hornpipe" is a fiddle tune that dates back to 1797, but many people know it today as part of Popeye the Sailor's theme song. Play the first part of it, below, to practice the A major scale:

"Sailors Hornpipe"

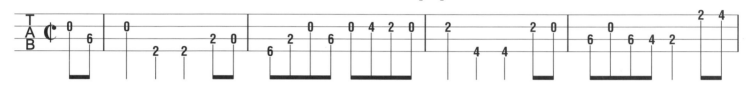

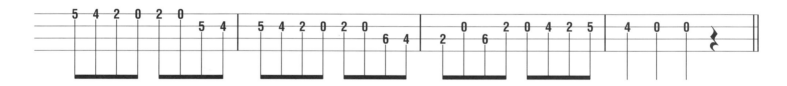

"SAWING" (FILLING OUT A MELODY)

Fiddlers sometimes embellish a melody by "sawing" on sustained notes, i.e. playing a note over and over in rhythm to fill out an empty space in a melody line. On a fiddle it looks like sawing wood when it's done with a bow, but mandolin players do the same thing by alternating upstrokes and downstrokes with a pick. For example, here are two versions of the first part of the old folk blues "Careless Love." One is the melody, the other includes "sawing."

"Careless Love"

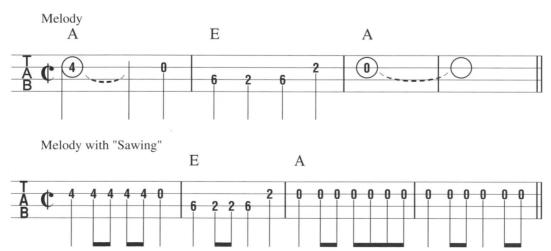

KEY OF C CHORDS

The C chord family is C (1), F (4), and G (5). The relative minors are Am, Dm, and Em. The only new chord shapes are F and Dm. Practice strumming them as shown below:

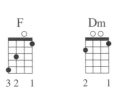
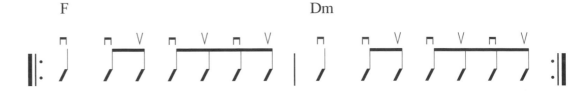

A 6/8 STRUM

The 6/8 strum is yet another rhythm groove found in many popular songs including "Hallelujah," "House of the Rising Sun," "Time Is on My Side," "Heart of Stone," "We Are the Champions," "How Can You Mend a Broken Heart," and "I Can't Help Falling in Love."

It consists mostly of downstrokes, with a few sixteenth notes to liven it up:

Strum a C chord:

⊓	⊓	V	⊓	⊓	⊓	⊓
1	2	and	3	4	5	6

Practice the strum by playing a few bars of "Hallelujah."

"Hallelujah"

[Tablature for "Hallelujah" with chords C, Am, C, Am and F, G, C, G]

ARPEGGIOS

When you play the notes of a chord one at a time, going up or down, it's called an *arpeggio*. Arpeggio playing can be an effective accompaniment—an alternative to strumming. The example on the top of the next page is a familiar example.

"House of the Rising Sun"—Arpeggios

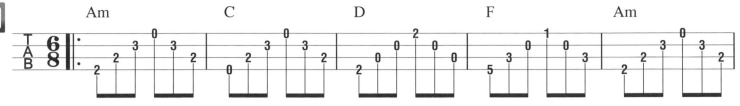

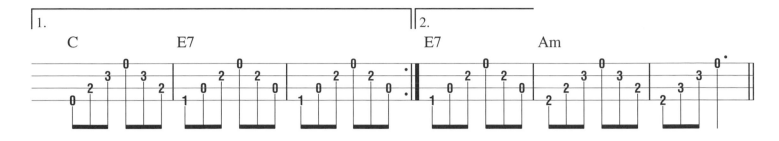

C MAJOR SCALE

When you practice the C major scale, you may notice that it contains the same notes as the G major scale, except there's an F instead of an F♯.

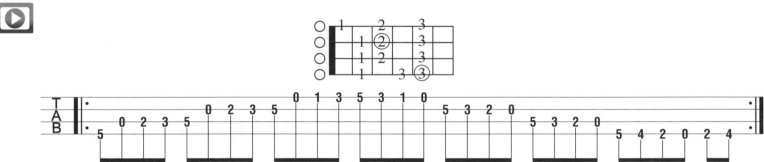

PLAYING A MELODY

"Wildwood Flower," made famous by the Carter Family, is well known to country and bluegrass pickers. The arrangement below will help you practice the C major scale.

"Wildwood Flower"

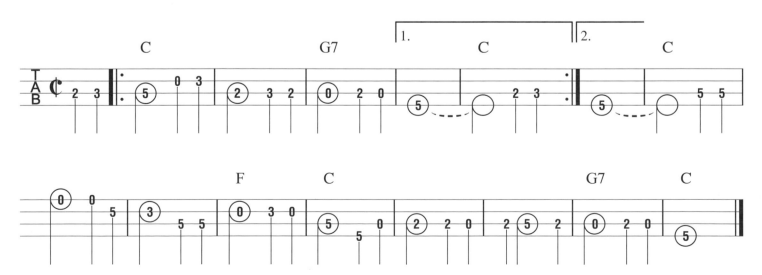

KEY OF E CHORDS

In the key of E, E is the 1 chord, A is 4, and B or B7 is 5. The relative minors are C#m, F#m, and G#m. The first string is muted when you play the easy B chord. To play the four-string B chord, you need to fret (barre) the two high pairs of strings with one finger, which some people find difficult. Here are the new chord shapes:

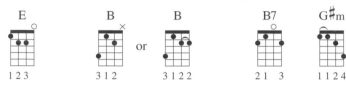

Play this chord progression to practice the new chords:

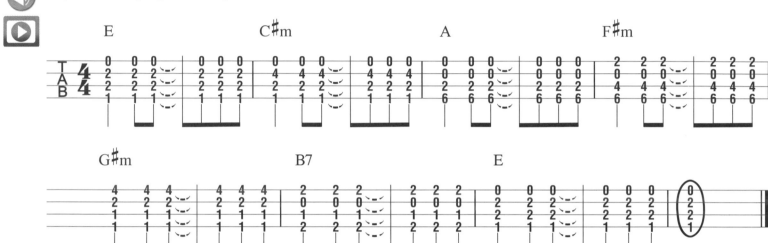

A WALTZ STRUM

Waltz tunes are in 3/4 time: three beats per bar instead of four or six. Some famous 3/4 songs include "The Tennessee Waltz," "Irene Goodnight," "Moon River," "Annie's Song," "Lara's Theme," "Piano Man," "Norwegian Wood," and "Happy Birthday to You."

Strum an E chord:

Practice the waltz strum by playing this early hit song written by Bill Monroe, the father of bluegrass music (and a famous mandolin player). The song was also a hit for Elvis Presley on his first (double-sided) hit record, although he changed it from a 3/4 waltz to a 4/4 boogie beat.

"Blue Moon of Kentucky"

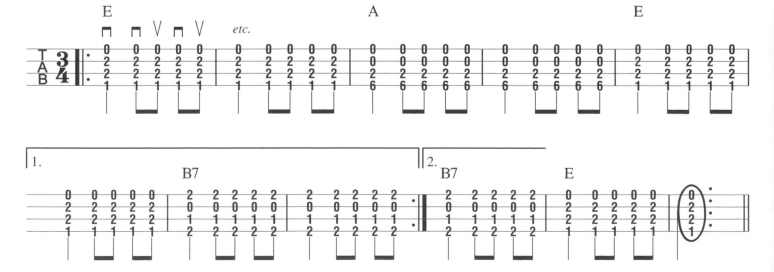

E MAJOR SCALE

The E major scale requires more use of the little finger than the other major scales you've encountered so far. Make sure you observe the fingering indicated by the fretboard diagram.

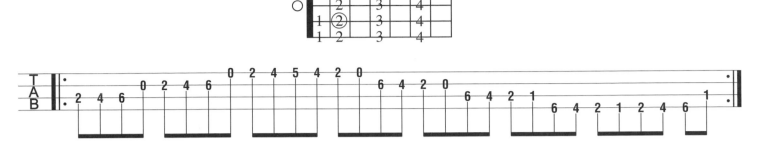

PLAYING A MELODY

The old folk song "Home on the Range" is written below as an exercise to practice the E major scale. Halfway through it jumps up an octave in order to make use of the mandolin's full range of E major scale notes.

"Home on the Range"

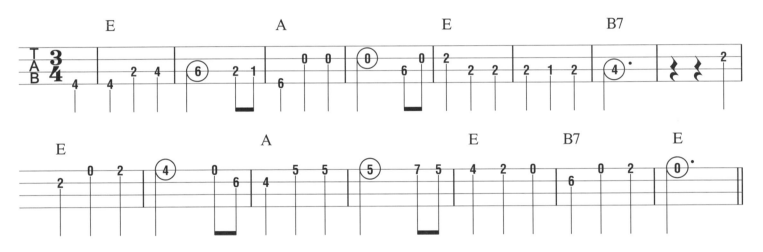

Here's another song to help you practice the E major scale. It's one you may be called upon to play quite often in social or professional situations. It's presented here in two octaves:

"Happy Birthday to You"

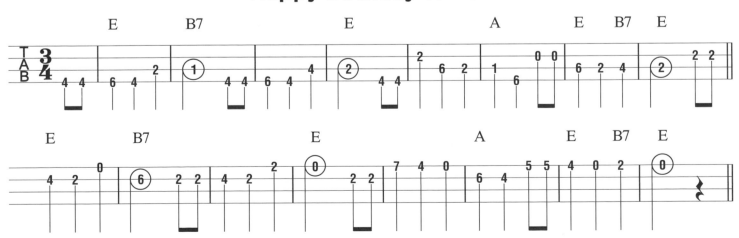

KEY OF F CHORDS

 In the key of F, F is the 1 chord, B♭ is the 4 chord, and C is the 5 chord. The relative minors are Dm, Gm, and Am. Here are the new chord shapes and an exercise to help you practice them. The progression is played with a rock ballad strum:

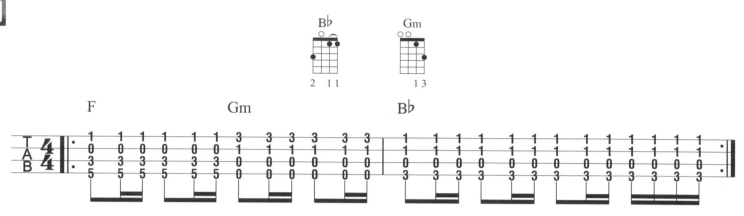

A LATIN/R&B STRUM

Many pop and R&B tunes feature variations of the straight-eighths groove that have a Latin feel. Here's an example that fits tunes like "Margaritaville," "Spanish Harlem," "Just My Imagination," "Under the Boardwalk," and "Stand by Me." Practice the strumming pattern and remember to alternate downstrokes and upstrokes, playing eight strokes per bar. To get the right rhythmic feel, you have to keep your hand moving and play those "ghost" strokes (the ones where you miss the strings). In this rhythm pattern, there's a "ghost" upstroke on the "and of 1" and another "ghost" downstroke on the third downbeat.

Strum an F chord: ⊓ — ⊓ V — V ⊓ V
                    1 and 2 and 3 and 4 and

Ben E. King's smash hit by Leiber and Stoller, "Stand by Me," was inspired by a gospel tune co-written by Sam Cooke and J. W. Alexander; it has been recorded by hundreds of artists. It features a simple four-bar progression that is shared with countless tunes. Here it is, played with a Latin feel.

"Stand by Me"

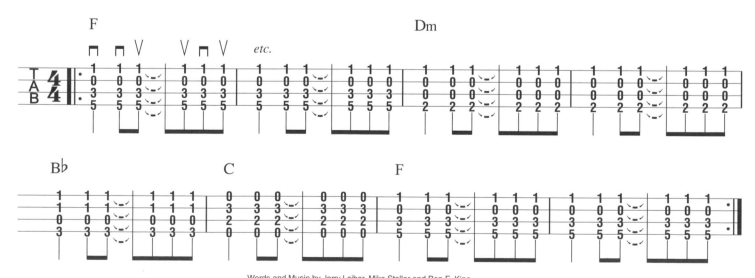

F MAJOR SCALE

Practice the F major scale as it's written below. Except for the B♭, it has the same notes as the C major scale.

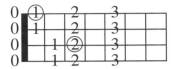

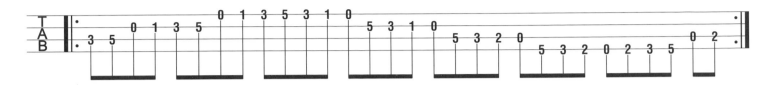

PLAYING A MELODY

Here's another old fiddle tune that'll give you a workout on the F major scale. At least two hundred years old, "Turkey in the Straw" is a bluegrass standard that has been featured in movies, cartoons, television shows, and video games; it has even been played over the loudspeakers of ice cream trucks!

"Turkey in the Straw"

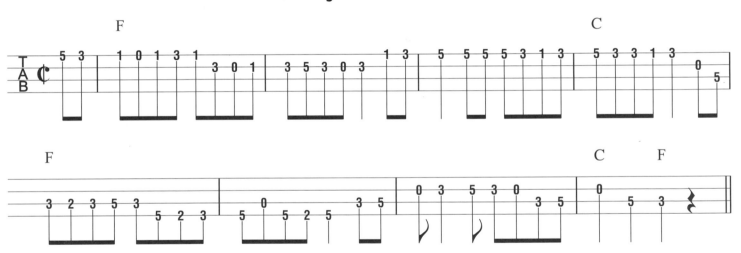

TREMOLO

Tremolo, that fast, fluttering sound of one or more notes being repeated rapidly, is one of the main distinguishing features of mandolin playing. It's the only way to sustain a note (or notes) for several beats, other than "sawing" (see Lesson 4). It's achieved by rapidly alternating upstrokes and downstrokes with a pick. Here are some examples:

While trying to duplicate the above samples, keep your wrist loose; all of the movement should be in the wrist, not the arm. It may be difficult to work up the speed necessary to make tremolo happen, but if you keep at it, the speed will come!

DOUBLE STOPS IN SEVERAL KEYS

A *double stop* is a musical term for two notes played simultaneously—in other words, a pair of notes. Mandolin players play occasional double stops to make solos sound richer and fuller, by supporting melody notes with harmony notes. Usually the melody note is higher in pitch than the harmonizing note.

Here are some double stops that can be played using easy first position chord shapes. Some of the double stops include notes outside of the chord shapes.

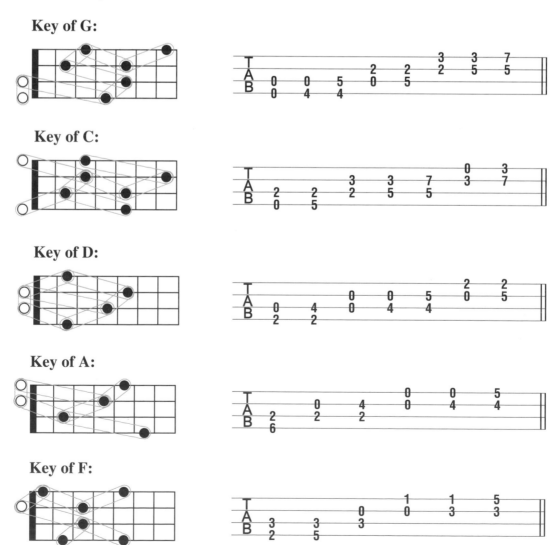

Learn these double stops one key at a time. Don't expect to memorize them all in one sitting! Practice the G, C, and D double stops and then play the following arrangement of the classic country tune "Will the Circle Be Unbroken."

"Will the Circle Be Unbroken"—with Double Stops and Sawing

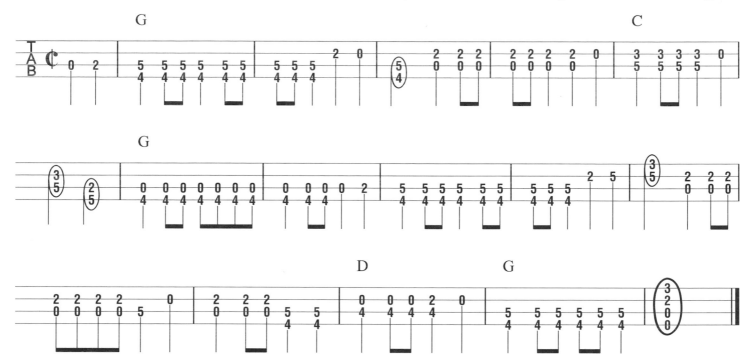

TREMOLO WITH DOUBLE STOPS

The two techniques (tremolo and double stops) are often combined, as seen in this alternate arrangement of "Will the Circle Be Unbroken." It's in the key of C, so practice your C (1), F (4), and G (5) double stops before playing it.

"Will the Circle Be Unbroken"—with Double Stops and Tremolo

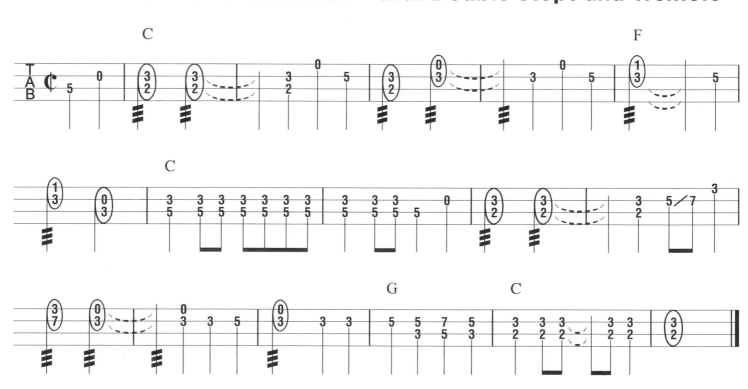

LESSON 9

CHOP CHORDS

 Chop chords are percussive, clipped chords that are played usually on the *backbeats* (the second and fourth beats in a bar of 4/4). They serve the same function as the snare drum in rock and other rhythmic musical genres. In bluegrass, chop chords are especially necessary to push the rhythm since bluegrass bands don't have drummers.

When playing chop chords, you mute the strings right after strumming a chord to get a staccato effect. This is done by lifting the fretting fingers slightly so that they still touch the strings but don't press down. That's why chop chords are moveable chords: chords that don't include open strings. The open strings would ring out and spoil the clipped effect.

Bluegrass players prefer the G- and C-shaped formations diagrammed below. Notice that the C chop chord can be played on three strings with the first string muted, or it can be played on all four strings—if you can manage it!

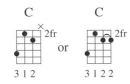

Practice the chop chords by playing some of the backup (accompaniment) to "I'll Fly Away," one of the most popular and most recorded gospel songs of all time.

"I'll Fly Away"

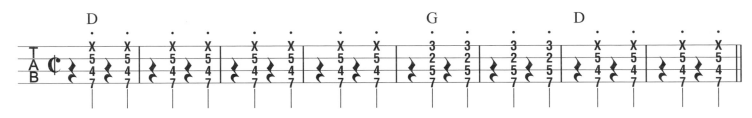

MOVEABLE CHOP CHORD FAMILIES

 It's easy to use chop chords to play chord families. There are two ways to do this: 1) using the G chop chord as the 1 chord, and 2) using the C chop chord as the 1 chord.

G chop chord/chord family (Key of G)

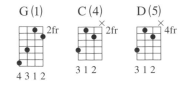

- Play the 4 chord by moving the 1 chord "up a string."

- Play the 5 chord by moving the 4 chord up two frets.

C chop chord/chord family (Key of D)

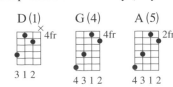

- Play the 5 chord by moving the 1 chord "down a string."

- Play the 4 chord by moving the 5 chord down two frets.

Play this 1–4–5 chord sequence from the Beatles' "Hey Jude" to practice the chord families—it's the part played over "Remember to let her into your heart..." and is presented below in the key of A and the key of D. Then try the sequence a few frets higher in the keys of B and E.

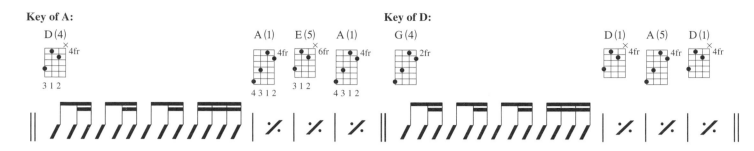

CHOP CHORD MAJOR SCALES

You can use the moveable chop chords as a springboard for moveable major scales, *which make it possible for you to solo all over the fretboard, in any key.* Here are two such scales:

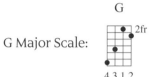
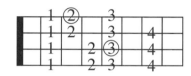

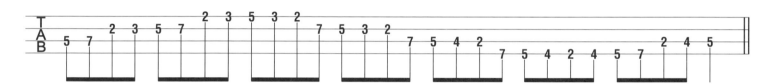

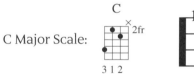

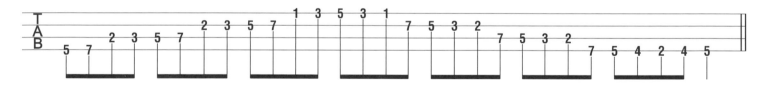

In the following version of "Wildwood Flower," the melody is based on the C chop chord/major scale played up two frets, putting it in the key of D.

"Wildwood Flower"

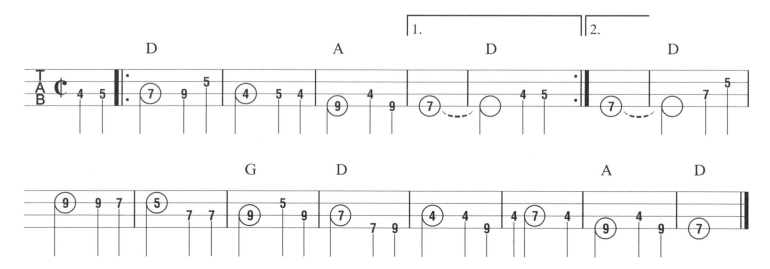

SEVENTH CHORDS

So far, you've played major chords and minor chords but few seventh chords. While major chords have a sunny, bright sound, and minor chords have a melancholy sound, seventh chords have a bluesy flavor and create *tension*. They sound like they want to go somewhere... and they do. In most popular music, the tension of a seventh chord is resolved by playing the chord that is a fourth higher (play G7 to C and listen for the "feeling of resolution"). Here are some first-position seventh chords:

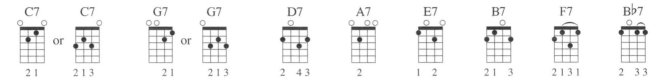

THE 12-BAR BLUES

Countless blues, early rock, and R&B songs share a popular progression known as the *12-bar blues*. Some examples include "Kansas City," "Hound Dog," "Johnny B. Goode," "Pride and Joy," "Crossroads," "I Can't Quit You, Baby," and so on. In blues tunes, the seventh chords don't always resolve up a fourth. In fact, all the chords are seventh chords and you even end on a seventh chord. Study the basic progression (it's made of three 4-bar phrases) and play the samples below while humming any of the above-mentioned tunes:

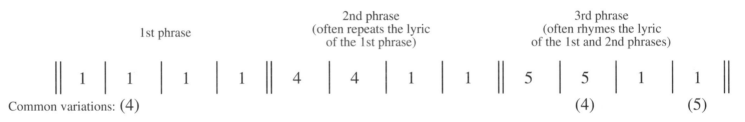

12-BAR BLUES IN TWO KEYS

Key of C: ‖ C7 | C7 | C7 | C7 ‖ F7 | F7 | C7 | C7 ‖ G7 | G7 | C7 | C7 ‖

Key of E: ‖ E7 | A7 | E7 | E7 ‖ A7 | A7 | E7 | E7 ‖ B7 | A7 | E7 | E7 ‖

BLUES SOLOING

In previous lessons you learned how to play first-position and moveable major scales. To play the blues you need to add some "blue notes" to your major scale-based licks, especially flatted 3rds and 7ths. Here are some *minor pentatonic blues scales* (five-note scales that include flatted 3rds and 7ths) to get you started improvising blues licks and solos. The root notes are circled.

Key of G:

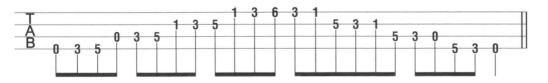

Key of C:

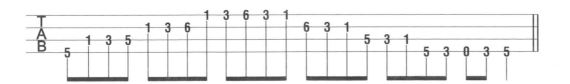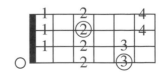

Key of D:

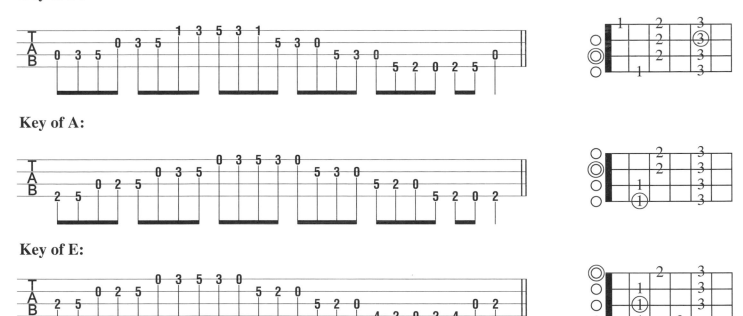

Key of A:

Key of E:

A scale is like an alphabet, but instead of putting letters together to make words, you put notes together to make licks and musical phrases. As demonstrated in the solos below, they can be short (two-note) or long phrases. Here's the beauty of the minor pentatonic scales: when you play the scale that matches your key (e.g., a C scale over the key of C), the ad-lib phrases you invent will work over all three chord changes (1, 4, and 5).

BLUES SOLOS

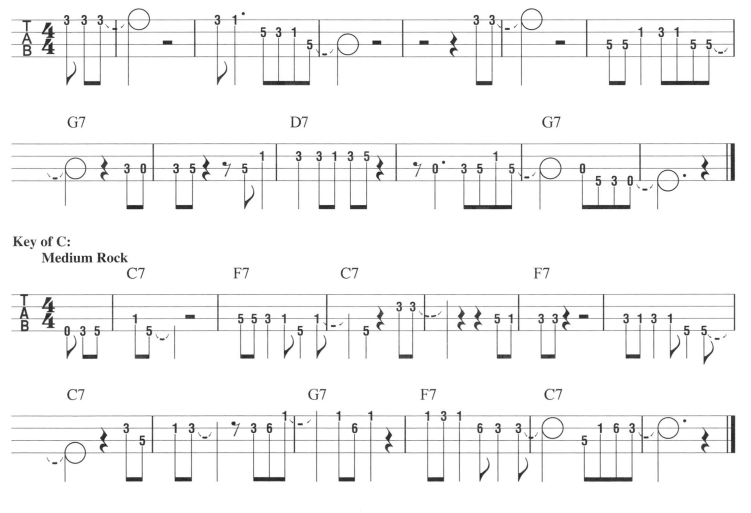

FANCIER CHORDS (FIRST POSITION)

So far, you've played major, minor, and seventh chords. But if you've worked through some popular music books, you've probably encountered more complicated chords (suspended, diminished, augmented, ninths, thirteenths...); and chords that look like chemistry formulas (G13♭9, B♭m7♭5, E6/G♯, and so on). Here are some facts about chords:

- *There are basically three types of chords*: major, minor, and seventh chords. Nearly all other chords are variations of one of those three types. For example, G13 is a G7 with one extra note added.

- Major chords have a bright, sunny sound, whereas minor chords often sound sad or melancholy.

- Seventh chords sound bluesy and hold tension, as if they want to lead somewhere. They usually resolve up a fourth (G7 leads to C, C7 leads to F, etc.).

- You can substitute simpler chords (major, minor, or sevenths) for those complex chords, if you stay within the type. For instance, you can play G7 instead of G13 and it will not sound wrong—it just won't sound as subtle. If you played a Gm instead of a G13, it would sound wrong. Still, it enriches your playing to know some of those "adult" chords. So, here are a few important ones:

Major 7ths

Major 7ths have a wistful sound. Here are a few easy first-position examples:

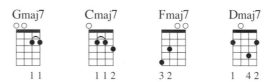

Diminished Chords

Diminished chords usually function as a bridge leading from one chord to another. Each diminished chord is made of four notes and can be named by any of the four. They also repeat every three frets. They're notated like this: Cdim or C°. A diminished chord is a seventh chord with every note lowered except the root. For example, to play a D° chord begin by fingering a first position D7 chord; then move every fretted string down a fret while retaining the open D/third string.

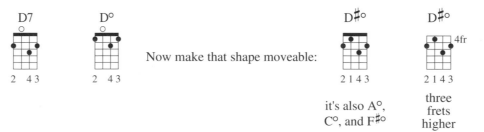

Augmented Chords

These chords have a lot of tension and repeat every four frets. They are written like this: E+.

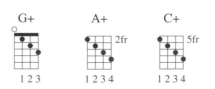

Minor 6ths

A minor chord with the 6th note of the scale added is called a minor 6th chord. They have a more plaintive sound than a plain minor chord:

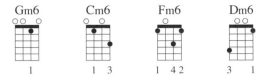

Suspended Chords

These chords actually do have a feeling of suspense. They usually resolve to their simpler form: Dsus4 is followed usually by D, G7sus4 usually comes before G7.

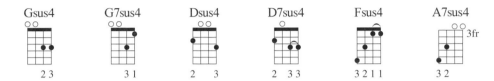

The great stride pianist, Fats Waller, wrote "Ain't Misbehavin'" in 1929. It makes use of several of the jazzy chords shown above. The first several bars resemble the beginning of several other songs including "Makin' Whoopee," "Tiptoe Through the Tulips," and "The Glory of Love."

"Ain't Misbehavin'"

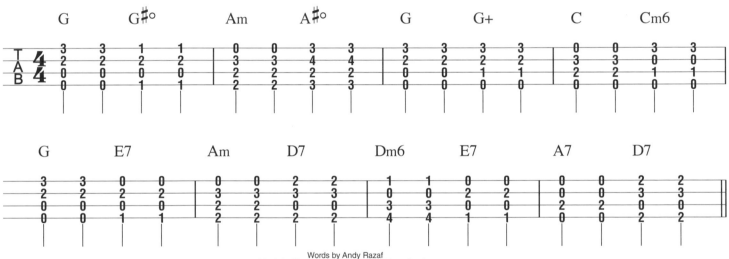

Words by Andy Razaf
Music by Thomas "Fats" Waller and Harry Brooks
© 1929 (Renewed) CHAPPELL & CO., INC., EMI MILLS MUSIC INC. and RAZAF MUSIC CO.
All Rights for EMI MILLS MUSIC INC. Administered by EMI MILLS MUSIC INC. (Publishing) and ALFRED MUSIC (Print)
All Rights for RAZAF MUSIC CO. Administered by BMG RIGHTS MANAGEMENT (US) LLC
All Rights Reserved   Used by Permission

 Here's a pop chord progression that makes use of major 7ths and suspended chords:

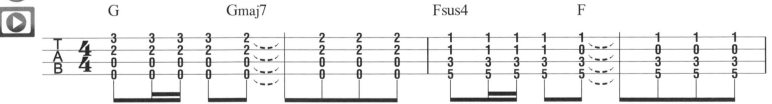

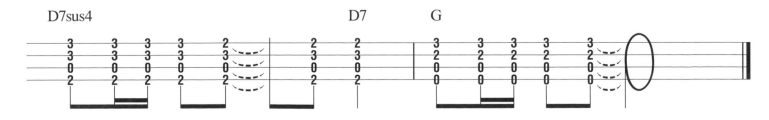

MOVEABLE CHORDS

In Lesson 9, you ventured up the neck with chop chords. In this lesson, we'll start playing other moveable shapes that enable you to play all over the mandolin fretboard in any key.

Most of the new chords are derived from first position chords you already know. Recognizing this connection will make it easier to remember the new shapes and make some sense out of them.

 These chord shapes are like the first position G, Gm, and G7 chords with a barre behind them:

The root of each chord shape is circled. If you know the notes on the fretboard, this helps you position the chord.

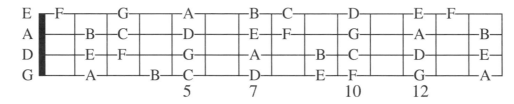

 These chord shapes are like a barred first position C, Cm, or C7 chord.

This seventh chord differs from the C chop chord by one note:

MOVEABLE CHORD FAMILIES

 If we group the moveable major chords into chord families, as we did the chop chords in Lesson 9, it makes playing tunes "up the neck" easier.

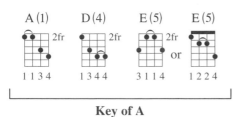

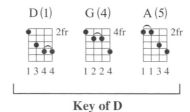

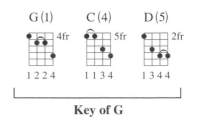

The popular song "Jamaica Farewell" can be played with the usual three chords: 1, 4, and 5, in that order. This makes it a good vehicle for practicing your moveable chord families. Here it is, played in three different keys:

"Jamaica Farewell"

Key of A:

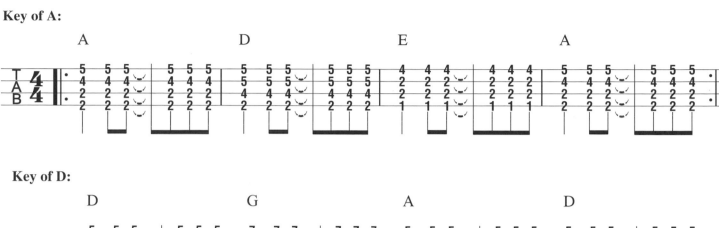

Key of D:

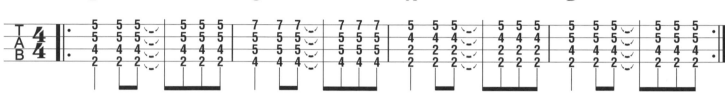

Key of G:

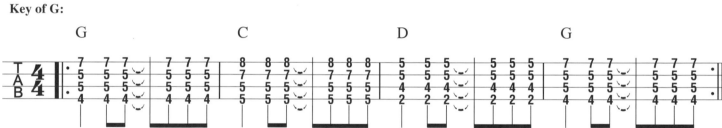

Here are the same 1-4-5 chord families in minor keys. Practice each chord family by strumming a 1-4-5 progression, like this:

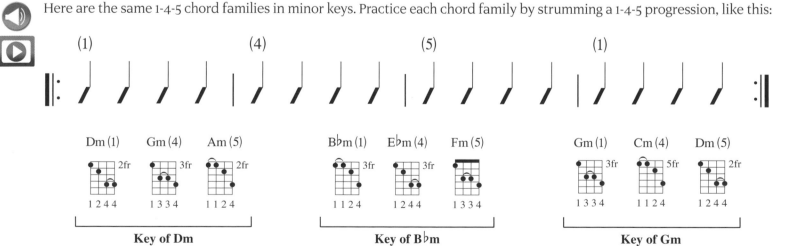

BLUES CHORDS: MOVEABLE 9THS AND 7THS

In Lesson 10, you learned the 12-bar blues format; you also learned that the blues often makes use of seventh chords instead of major chords. The moveable chords written below will enable you to play blues songs in any key, all over the fretboard. Notice that there are ninth chords as well as seventh chords. These two types of chords are interchangeable since a ninth chord is just a fancier seventh chord (a seventh chord with one extra note added).

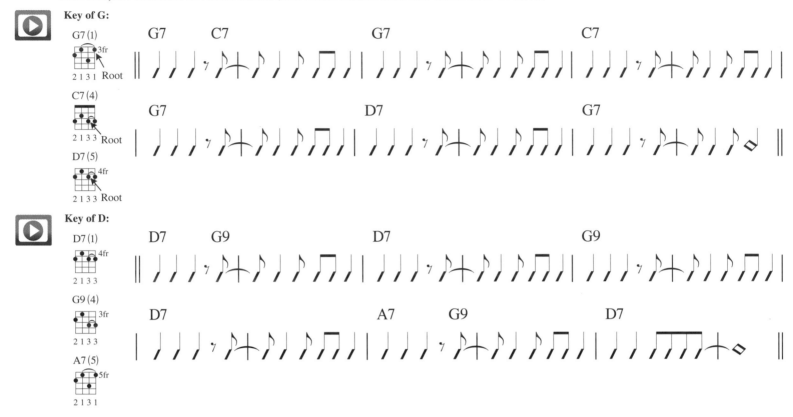

MOVEABLE BLUES CHORD FAMILIES

Here's how you can arrange these chords into moveable chord families:

The same configurations happen regardless of key; the relationships between the 1, 4, and 5 chords are constant. For example, in both moveable chord families the 4 chord is a fret lower than the 1 chord, and the 5 chord is always two frets higher than the 4 chord.

Here are the chord changes to "(They Call It) Stormy Monday (Stormy Monday Blues)," a 12-bar blues made famous by T-Bone Walker, the man who's most responsible for electrifying blues guitar playing. It's written below in the key of A:

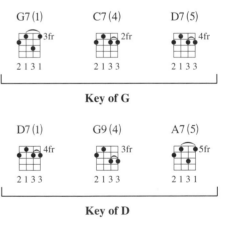

"(They Call It) Stormy Monday (Stormy Monday Blues)"

Key of A:

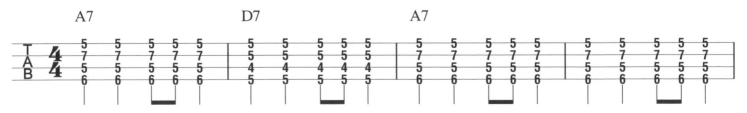

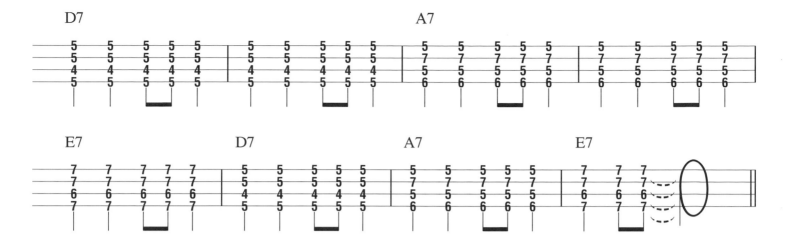

You can move the key-of-A "(They Call It) Stormy Monday (Stormy Monday Blues)" down two frets to play it in the key of G.

MOVEABLE MINOR PENTATONIC SCALES

In Lesson 10, you used first position minor pentatonic scales to solo in the lower part of the fretboard. Now, you'll learn some moveable minor pentatonic scales (sometimes called *blues boxes*) that you can use to solo in any key, all over the fretboard. Both scales are based on the chop chords you learned in Lesson 9. You don't have to play the chop chords while playing the scales; just hover over them and use them as reference points.

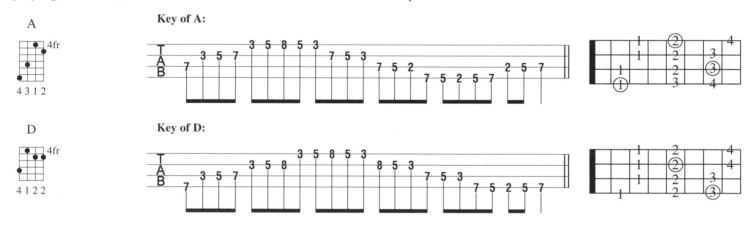

You can ad lib blues solos using these minor pentatonic scales, just as you did in Lesson 10. The licks you invent will work over all three chord changes in "(They Call It) Stormy Monday (Stormy Monday Blues)" or in other countless blues songs. *You can also use the blues boxes for any song in a minor key, or in any blues, rock, or country song in which the singer is singing "blue notes."*

"12-Bar Blues Solo"

Key of A:

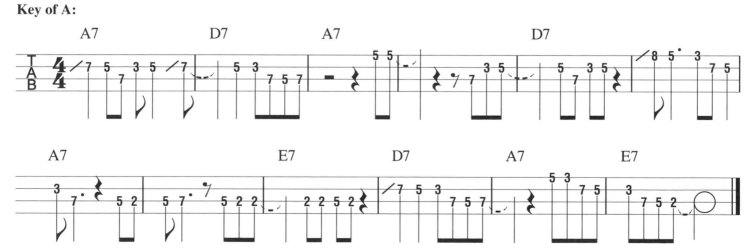

NAVIGATING THE CIRCLE-OF-FIFTHS

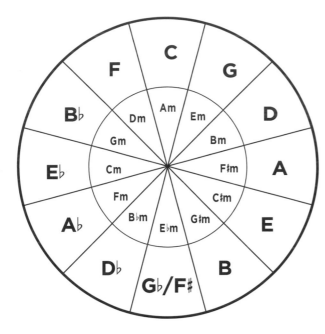

The chart pictured here is the key to understanding how chord progressions work in countless songs. Let's see what secrets it holds, and then apply them to the mandolin!

The circle-of-fifths chart includes all 12 tones (A, B♭, B, C, D♭, etc.) in a particular order. A step clockwise takes you up a fifth (e.g., from C to G) and a step counterclockwise takes you up a fourth (e.g., from C to F). As a result, the chart groups chords in their 1-4-5 chord families. Look at the C chord at the top of the chart; its 5 chord (G) is to the right and its 4 chord (F) is to the left. This is true of any chord you pick. The chords inside the circle are relative minors (e.g., Am, the relative minor of C, is placed directly beneath the C chord).

Chord progressions often move up by fourths, counterclockwise around the circle. Typically, if a progression jumps out of the chord family, you step up by fourths to return to the 1 chord. For example, in the first eight bars of "Five Foot Two, Eyes of Blue" (and many other songs) you jump from C (the 1 chord) to E or E7; you then return to the 1 chord by playing seventh chords counterclockwise around the circle:

$$\| \quad C \quad | \quad E7 \quad | \quad A7 \quad | \quad A7 \quad | \quad D7 \quad | \quad G7 \quad | \quad C \quad | \quad C \quad \|$$

THE RHYTHM CHANGES

As you ascend by fourths, the chords along the way may be minors instead of sevenths. One of the most often used circle-of-fifths progressions is the "Rhythm Changes," named after George Gershwin's "I Got Rhythm." It's 1, 6-, 2-, 5, or, in the key of C:

$$\begin{array}{cccc} C & Am & Dm & G7 \\ \| \quad 1 & 6- & | \quad 2- & 5 \quad \| \end{array}$$

Am is the 6 chord because A is the sixth note in the C major scale; Dm is the 2 chord because D is the second note in the C major scale, and so on. Because so many popular songs include the "Rhythm Changes" ("Blue Moon," "Be My Baby," "Heart and Soul," "Stand by Me," etc.) it's a good idea to learn how to play this progression in several keys:

Key of G:

G	Em	Am	D7

```
    3  3  3 3 3     0    0    2 2 2 2
T 4 2  2  2 2 2     0    0    3 3 3 3
A 4 0  0  0 0 0     2    2    0 0 0 0
B   0  0  0 0 0     2    2    2 2 2 2
```

Key of D:

D	Bm	Em	A7

```
    2  2  2 2 2     3  3    0 0 0
    0  0  0 0 0     2  2    0 0 0
    0  0  0 0 0     2  2    2 2 2
    2  2  4 4 4     0  0    0 0 0
```

The popular 1950s song "Mister Sandman" jumps nearly halfway around the circle (in the key of C, that's from C to B7), and then moves counterclockwise, ascending by fourths and using seventh chords to get back to C (the 1 chord).

"Mister Sandman"

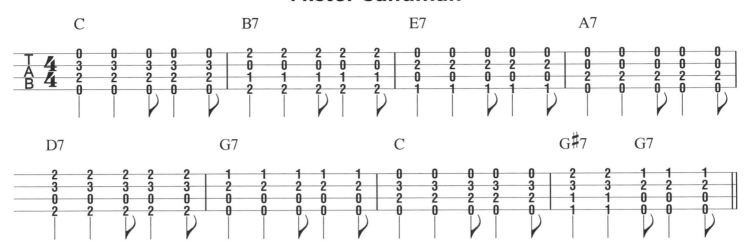

There's a circle-of-fifths progression that's the template for countless blues and swing songs like Robert Johnson's "They're Red Hot," "Ja-da," and "Keep on Truckin' Mama." Every 1930's blues guitarist had a song in this format, and Arlo Guthrie used it in his hit, "Alice's Restaurant." It breaks down like this:

$$\| 1 \quad 6 \mid 2 \quad 5 \quad 1 \mid 1 \quad 6 \mid 2 \quad 5 \mid 1 \quad 1^7 \mid 4 \quad 4\text{- or 1 dim.} \mid 1 \quad 6 \mid 2 \quad 5 \quad 1 \|$$

Here it is, in the key of C:

"They're Red Hot"

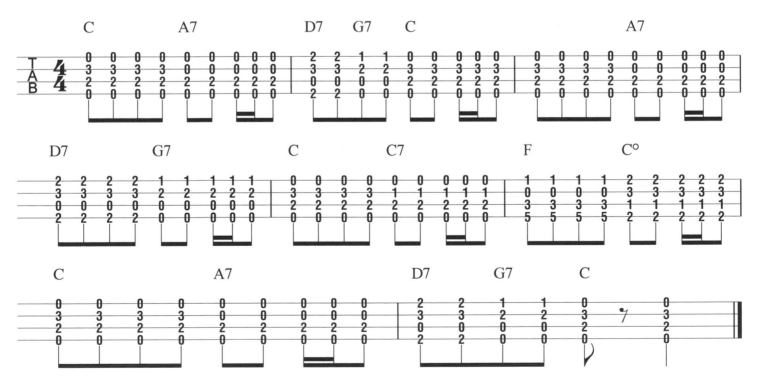

CHORD/MELODY PLAYING

 So far, you've learned some accompaniment strums and several single- and double-note soloing strategies. On the mandolin, it's also possible to play chords and melody at the same time in order to play a fuller arrangement, like a guitarist or pianist. Here are a few guidelines:

- You don't need to play a chord with every melody note, but each chord change should be played at least once during a bar of music.

- A melody note stands out better when it's the highest note of a chord.

- To support high, medium, and low melody notes you need to know several ways to play any chord: in first position and a few up-the-neck positions.

- Sometimes you may have to invent a unique voicing to support a melody note with a chord. That includes partial (two- or three-note) chords.

 The first step in creating a chord/melody solo is learning the melody; then you add the chords. Here's an easy example using the old (1869!) drinking song "Little Brown Jug," which was the basis for Chuck Berry's biggest hit, "My Ding-a-ling." Here's the melody:

"Little Brown Jug"—Melody

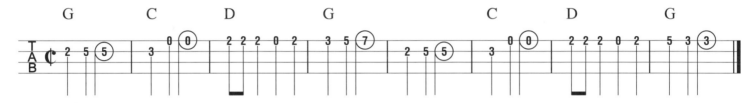

 Now, we'll add the chords:

"Little Brown Jug"—Chord/Melody Arrangement

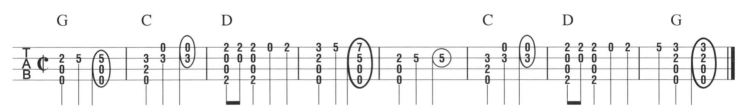

Notice that the first string is not played in the initial G chord. This is because the second string contains the melody note, and we want that to be the highest note. Also notice that the second G chord in the fourth bar is a higher voicing. By using this chord we're able to support that high melody note on the 7th fret of the first string.

More complicated tunes require more sophisticated arrangements, using subtle chords and up-the-neck or unusual voicings of chords. For example, take a close look at this arrangement of "The Godfather (Love Theme)."

"The Godfather (Love Theme)"

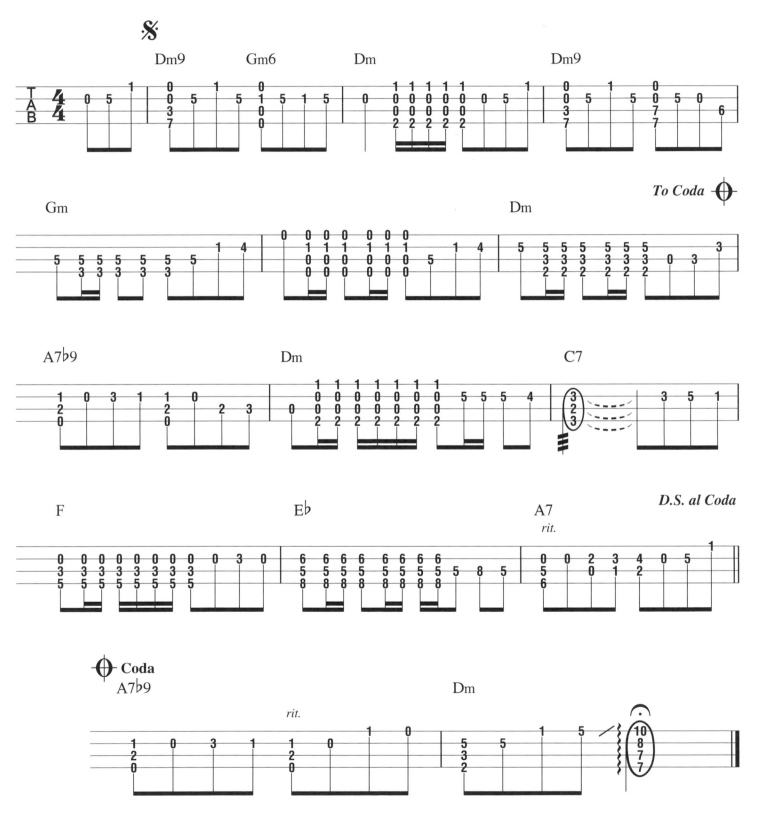

ABOUT THE AUTHOR

Fred Sokolow is best known as the author of over 150 instructional and transcription books and videos for guitar, banjo, Dobro, mandolin, lap steel, and ukulele. Fred has long been a well-known West Coast multi-string performer and recording artist, particularly on the acoustic music scene. The diverse musical genres covered in his books and DVDs, along with several bluegrass, jazz, and rock CDs he has released, demonstrate his mastery of many musical styles. Whether he's playing Delta bottleneck blues, bluegrass, or old-time banjo or mandolin, '30s swing guitar, or screaming rock solos, he does it with authenticity and passion.

Fred's other mandolin books include:

- *Fretboard Roadmaps for Mandolin*, book/sound files (with Bob Applebaum), Hal Leonard

- *First 50 Songs You Should Play on Mandolin*, Hal Leonard

- *101 Mandolin Tips*, book/sound files, Hal Leonard

- *Masters of the Mandolin*, Hal Leonard

Email Fred with any questions about this or his other mandolin books at: **Sokolowmusic.com**.